I0476915

Rebecca Page's
Patterns for Artists

Patterns with Shapes

Written by Joyce Page

Illustrated by Rebecca Page

Rebecca Page's Patterns for Artists: Patterns with Shapes

Copyright © 2009 by Rebecca Page

All rights reserved. No part of this book may be reproduced or transmitted in any form or by any means without written permission from the author.

ISBN 978-1512258240

Printed in USA by Create Space

Rebecca Page's Patterns for Artists offers an adventure in art, or an escape into colors. Each design provides a variety of fascinating possibilities for exploring shapes, patterns and colors. You can work in a random pattern or you may find pleasure in repeating your patterns. You can use crayons, colored pencils, water paints, pastels, markers or a mix of all to create your own art. Bold and bright colors are Rebecca's favorite, but you can choose bold, bright colors or lighter, shades of color, or a mix of both.

No two patterns are alike, and you as an artist will make your own unique Pattern art. All ages and abilities can create beautiful art using these patterns and their own choice of colors.

Created by Self Advocate artist Rebecca Page, who has Down syndrome, Patterns for Artists is unique among coloring books. Inspired by a support worker who enjoyed coloring Mandalas, Rebecca has found coloring patterns to be calming and relaxing to the soul. Enjoyed by her friends, patterns are an art that lets you escape wherever your imagination directs you. Creating Pattern Art to share with other aspiring artists has been a new and exciting project for Rebecca.

Young and old, different abled, or not, you will enjoy your time spent coloring Rebecca's Patterns for Artists. Spend hours coloring beautiful patterns!

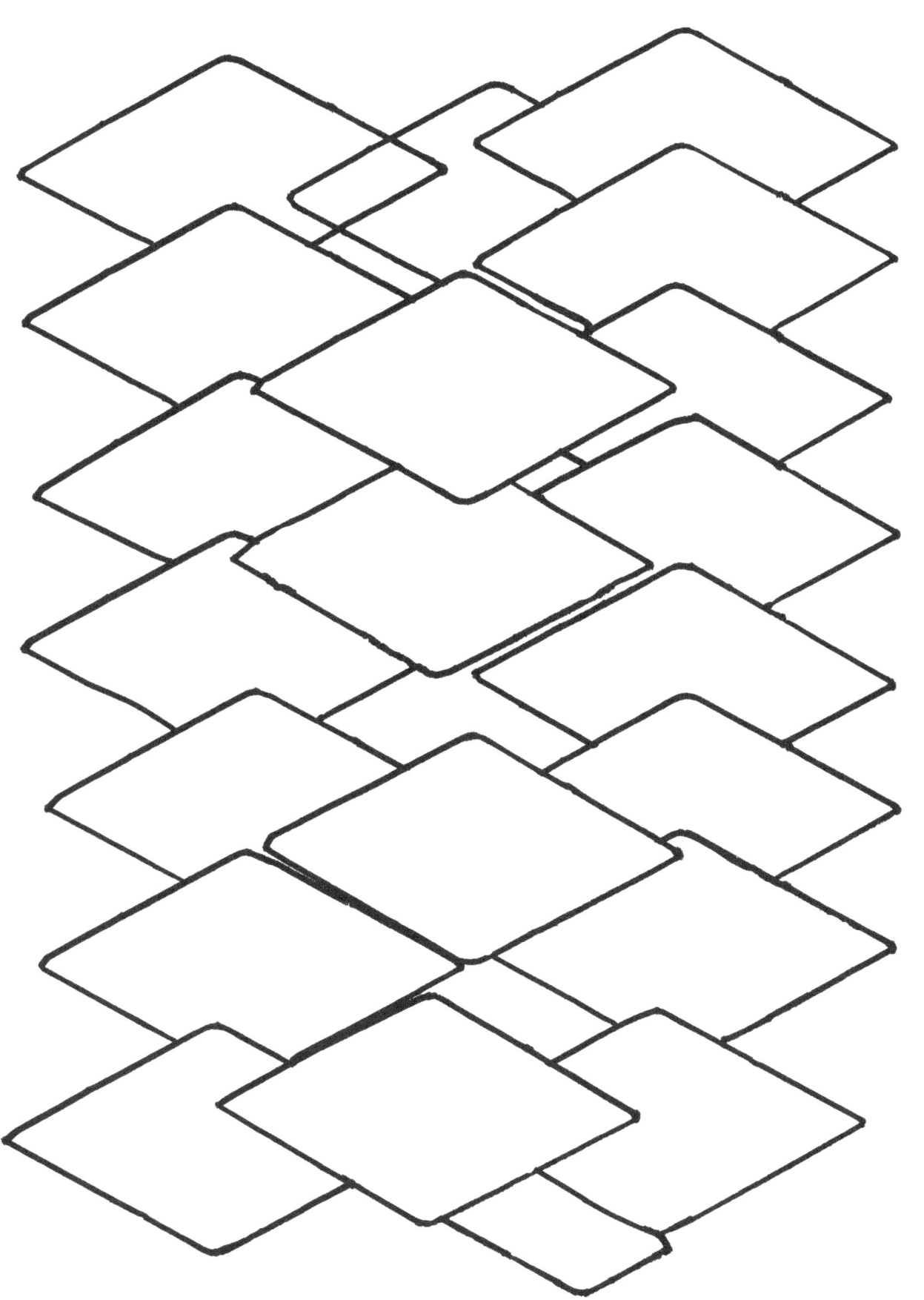

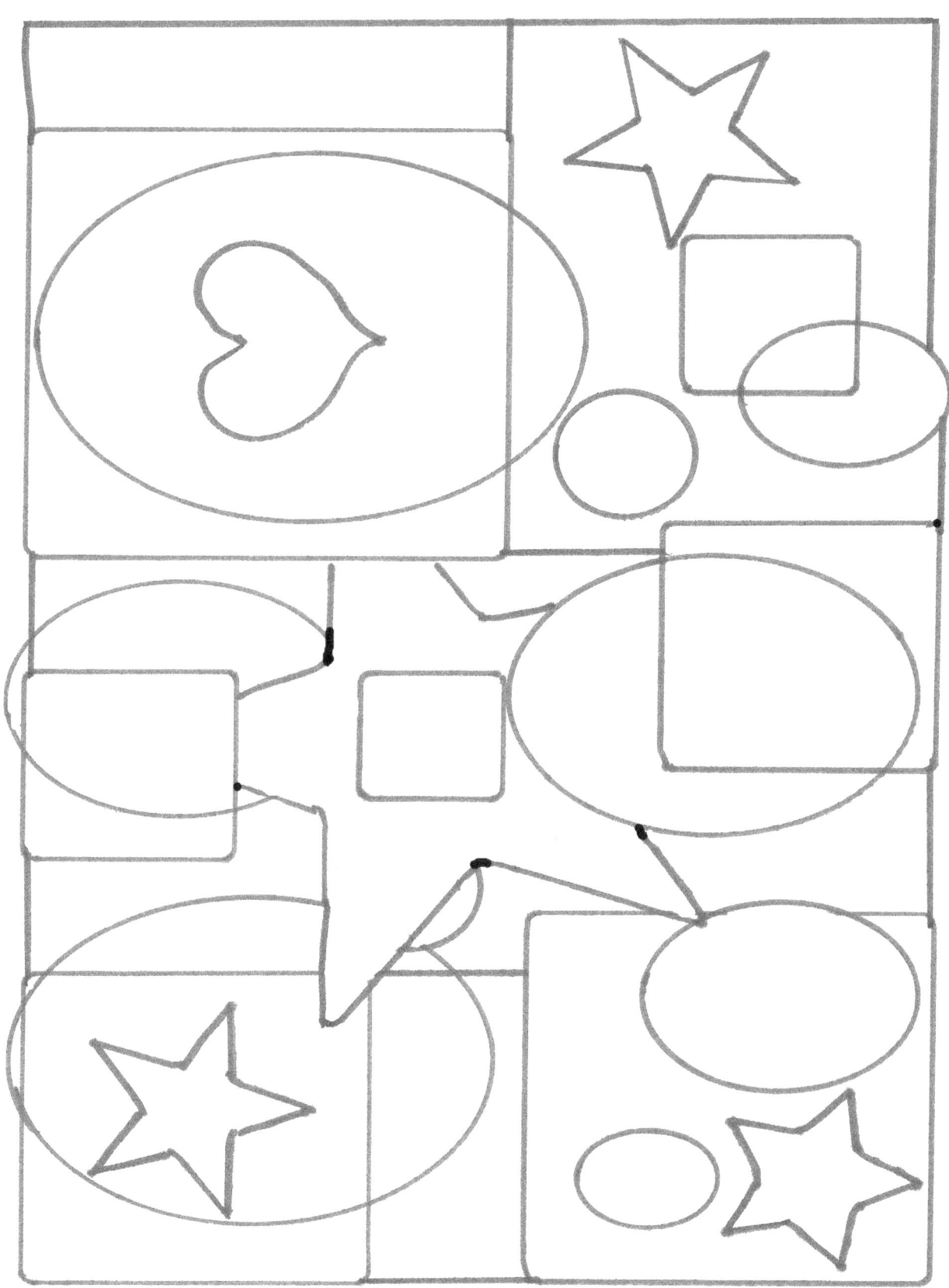

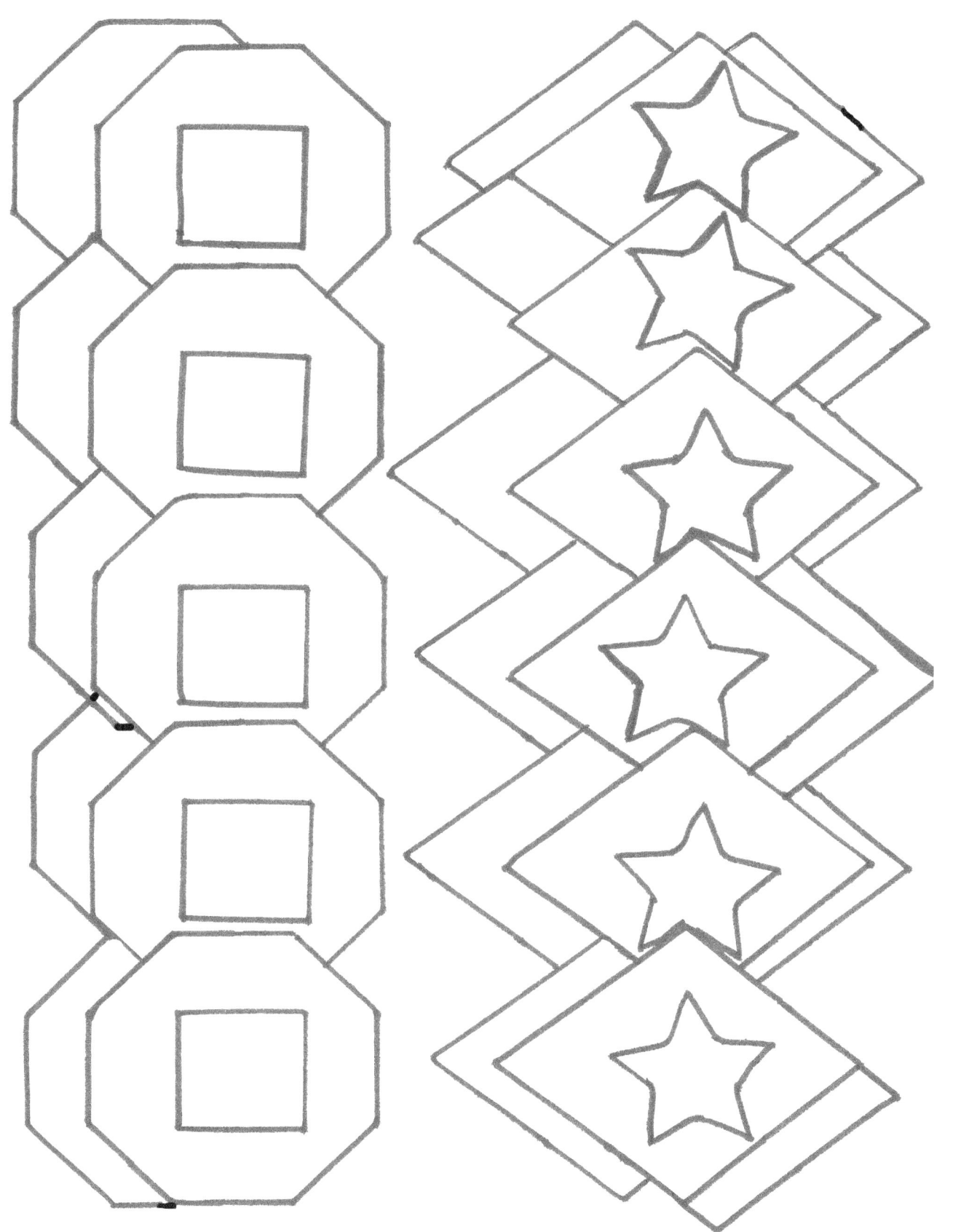

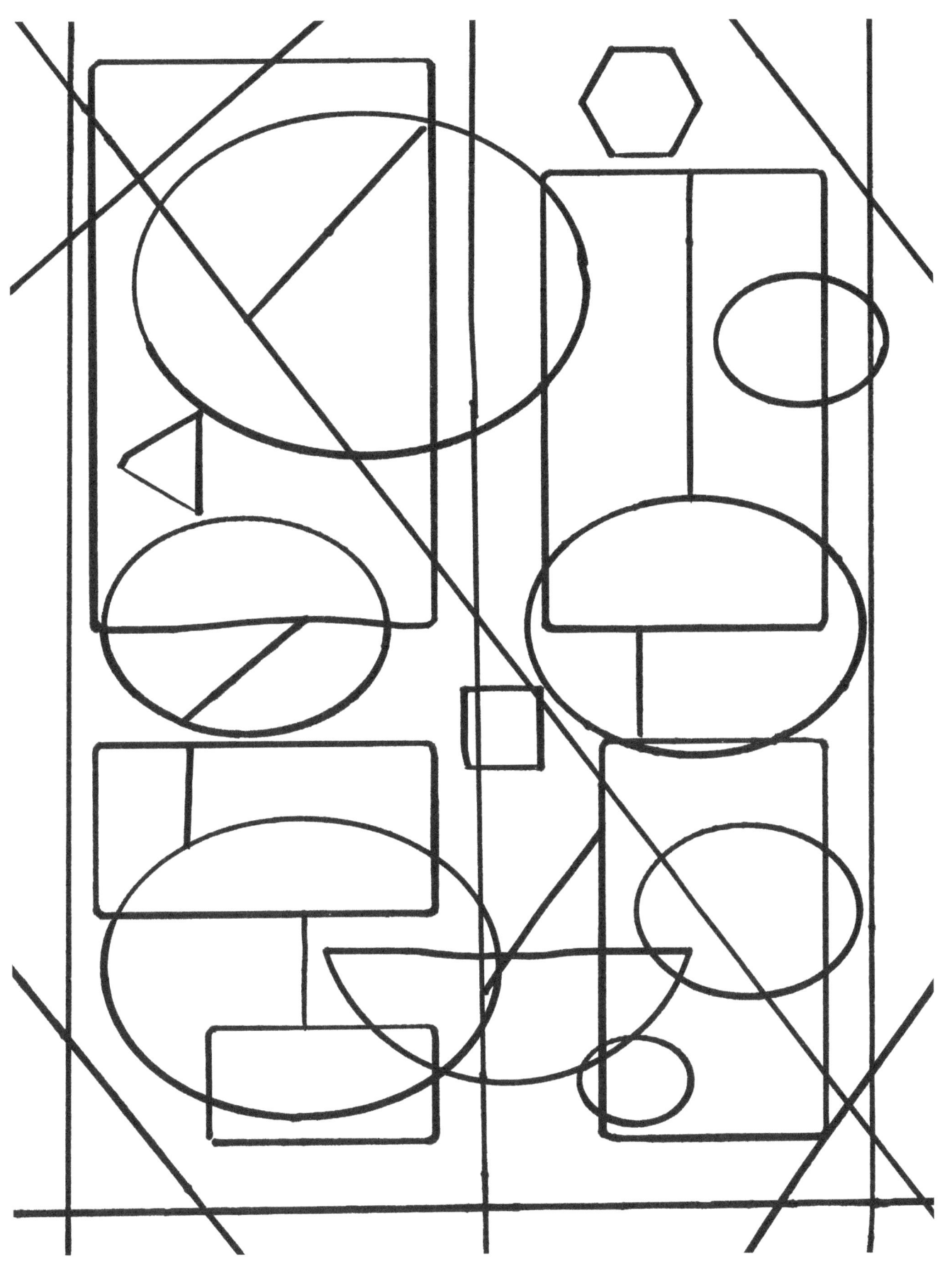

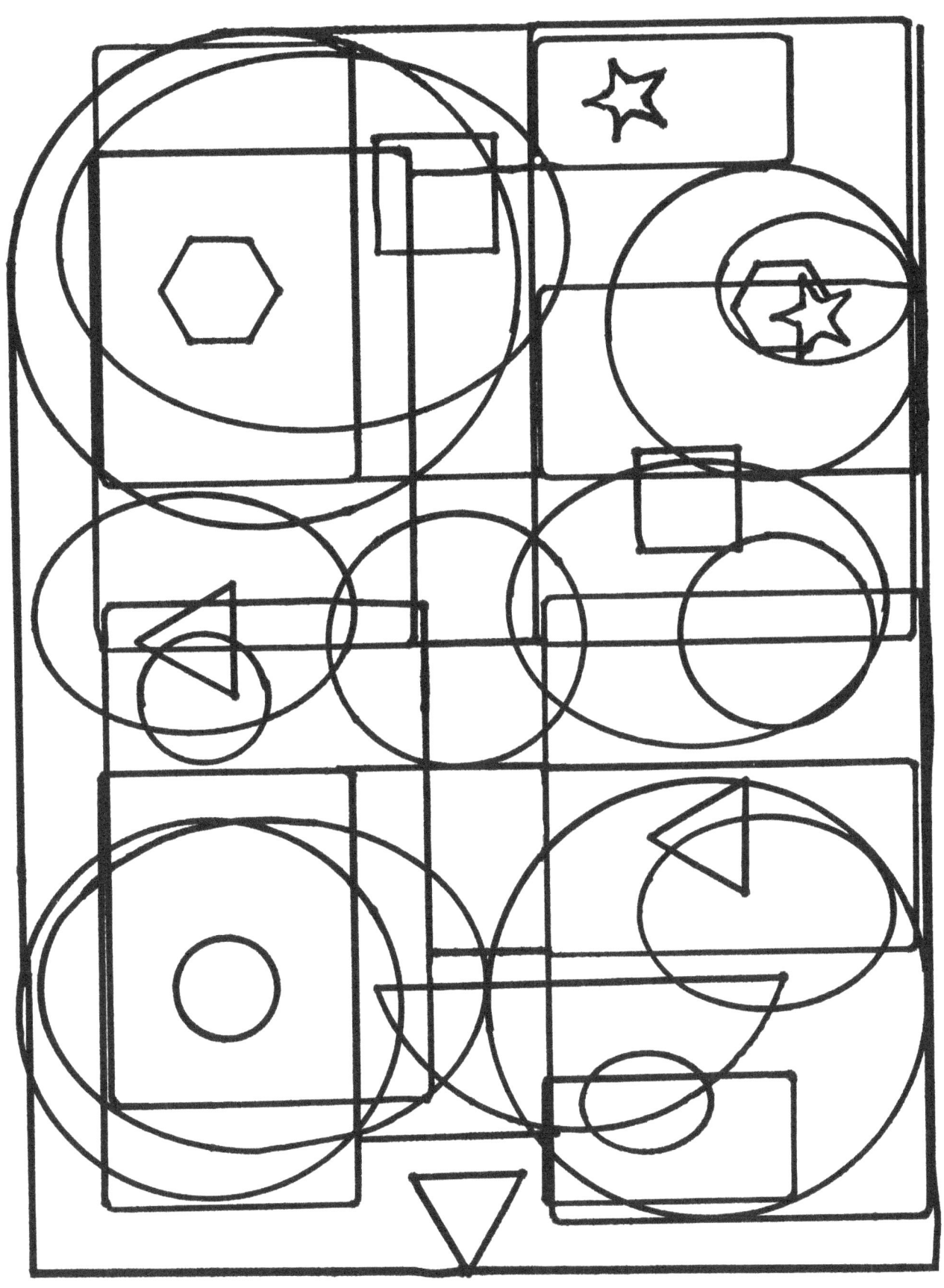

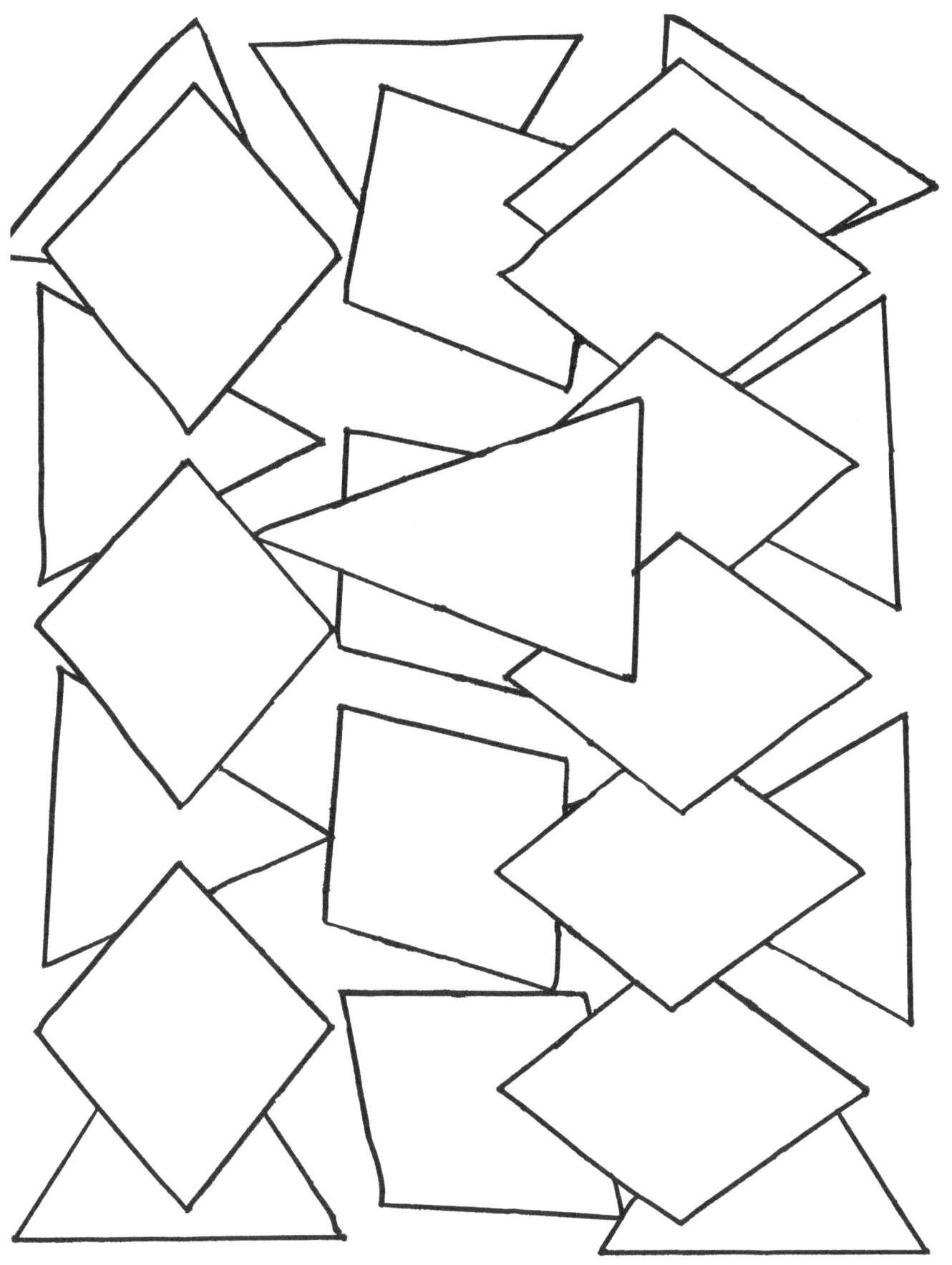

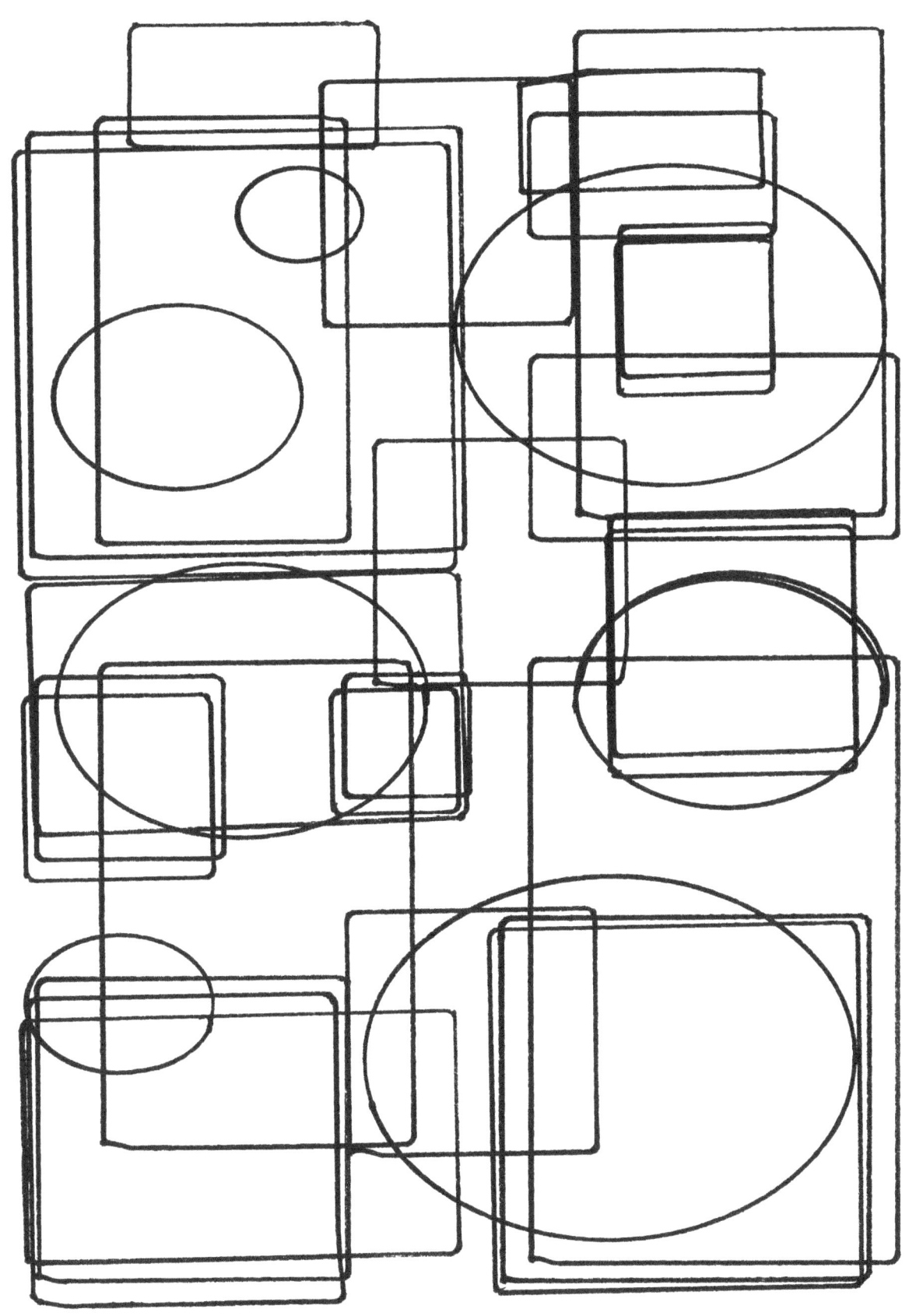

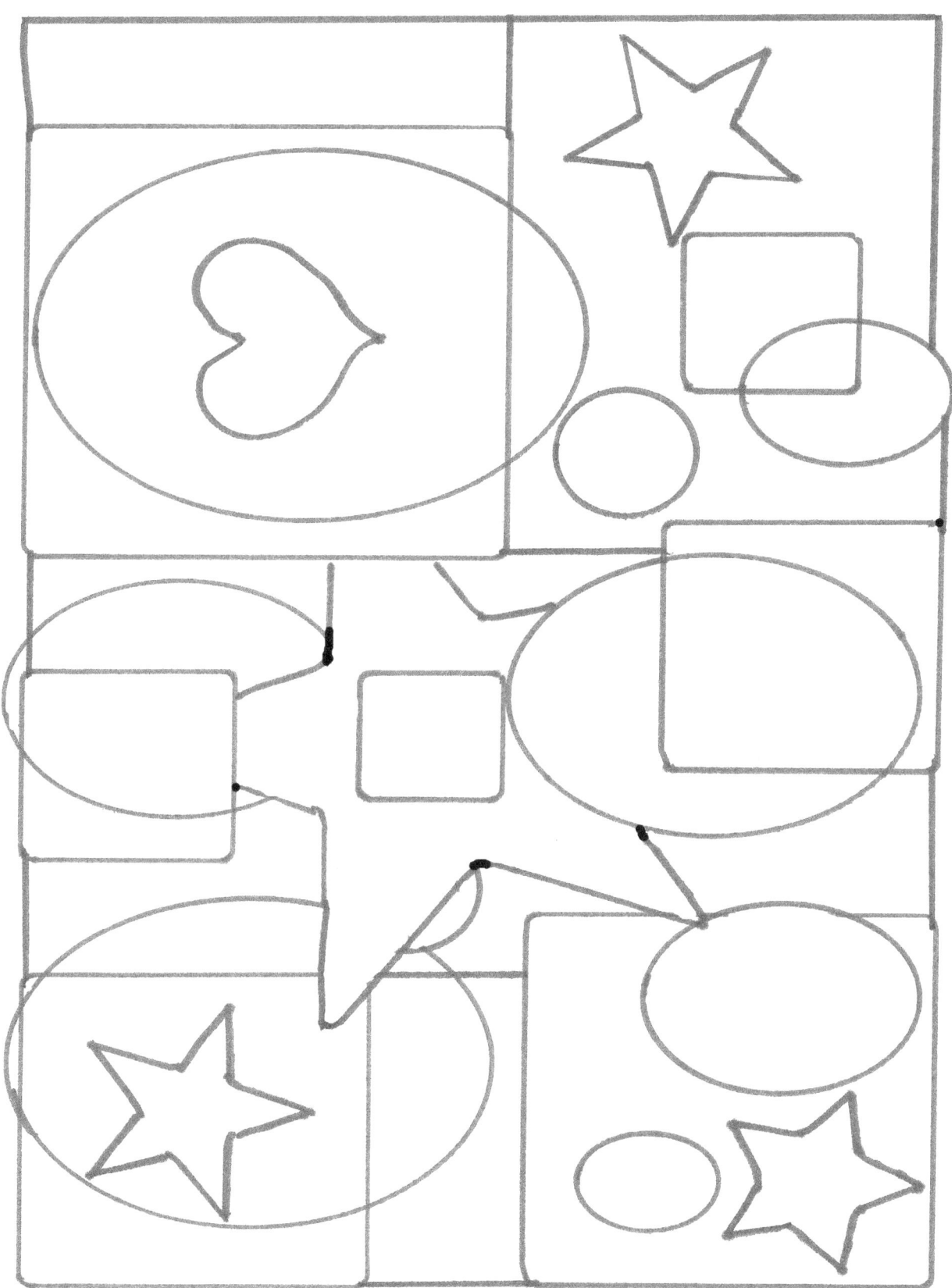

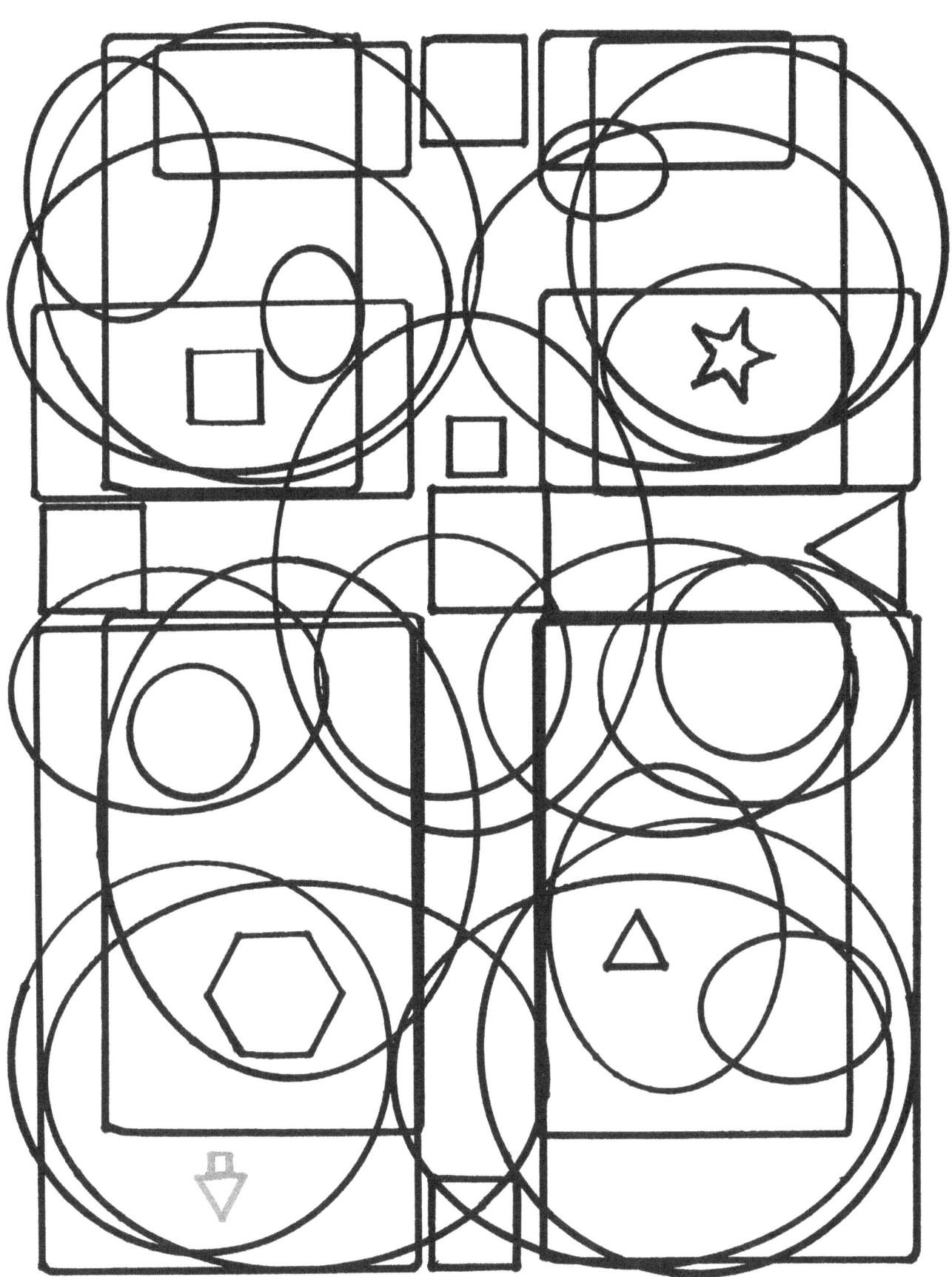

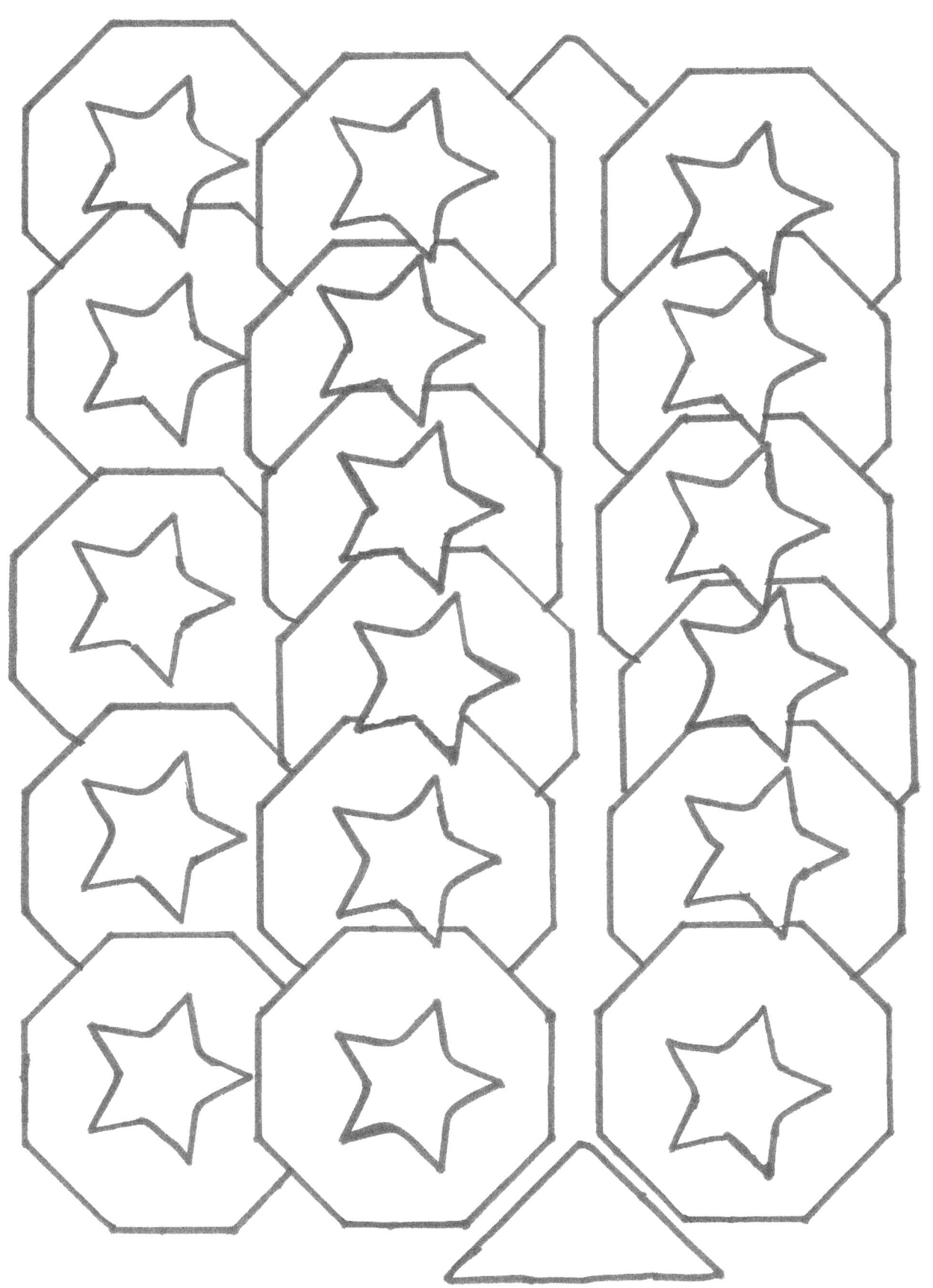

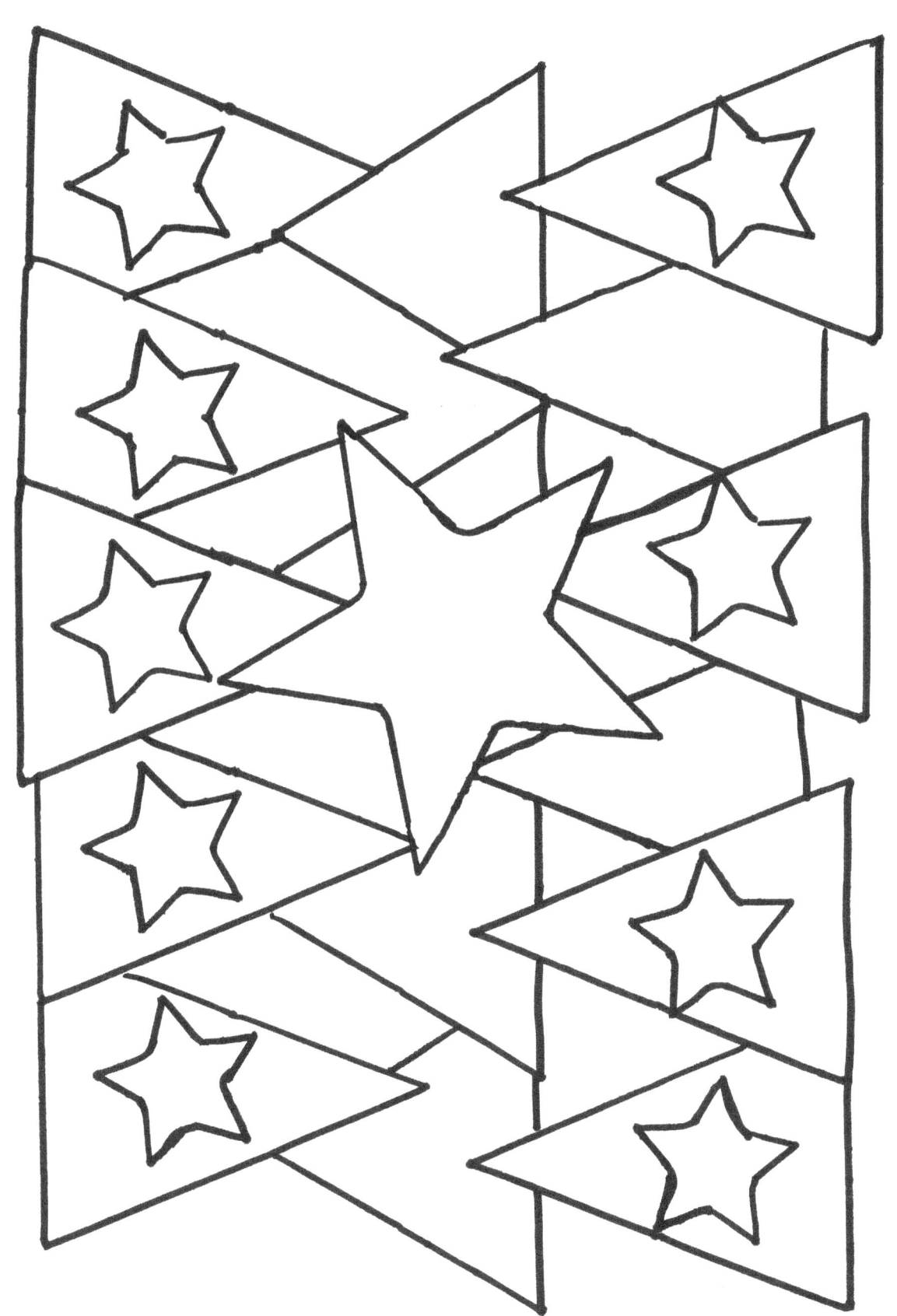

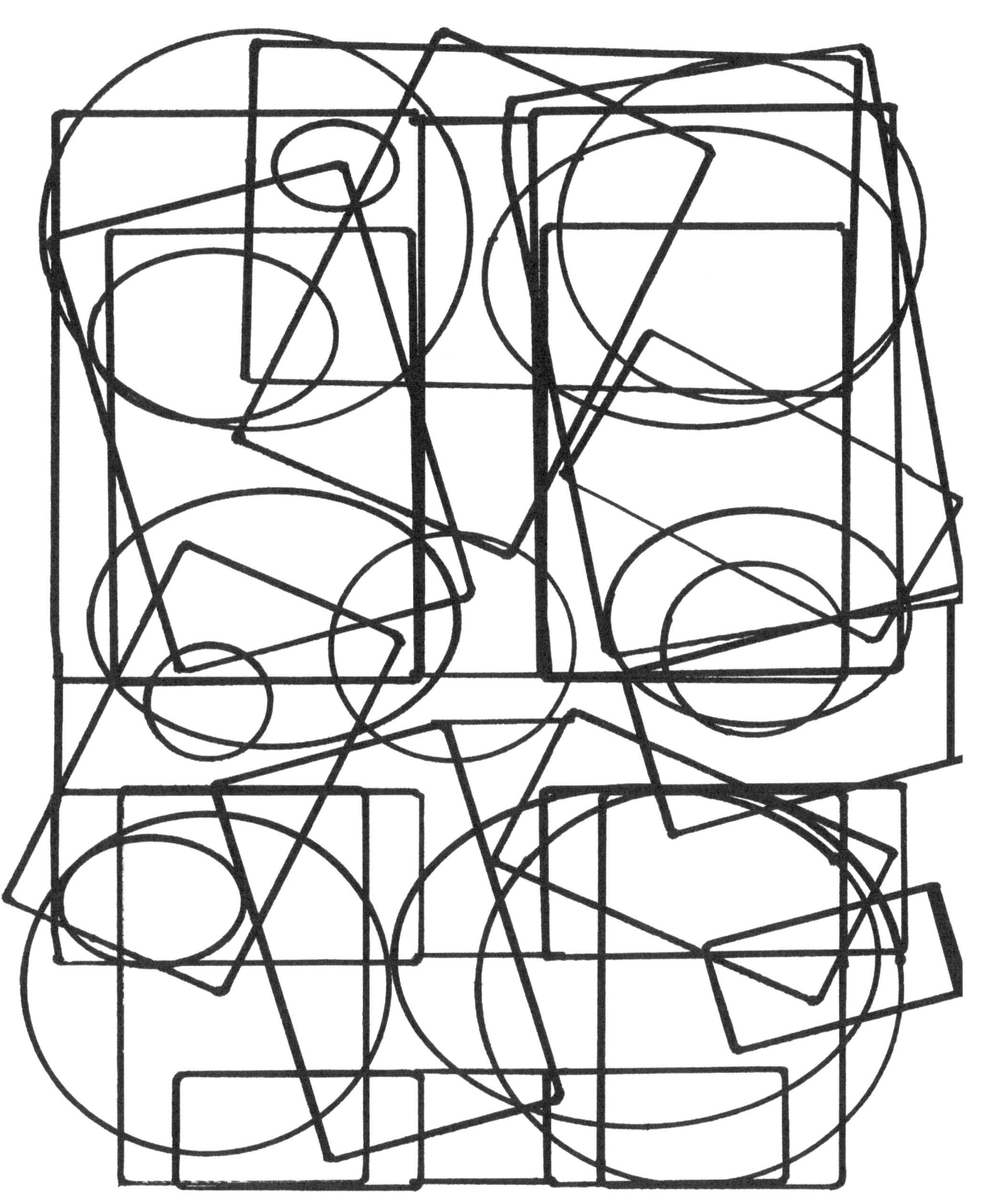

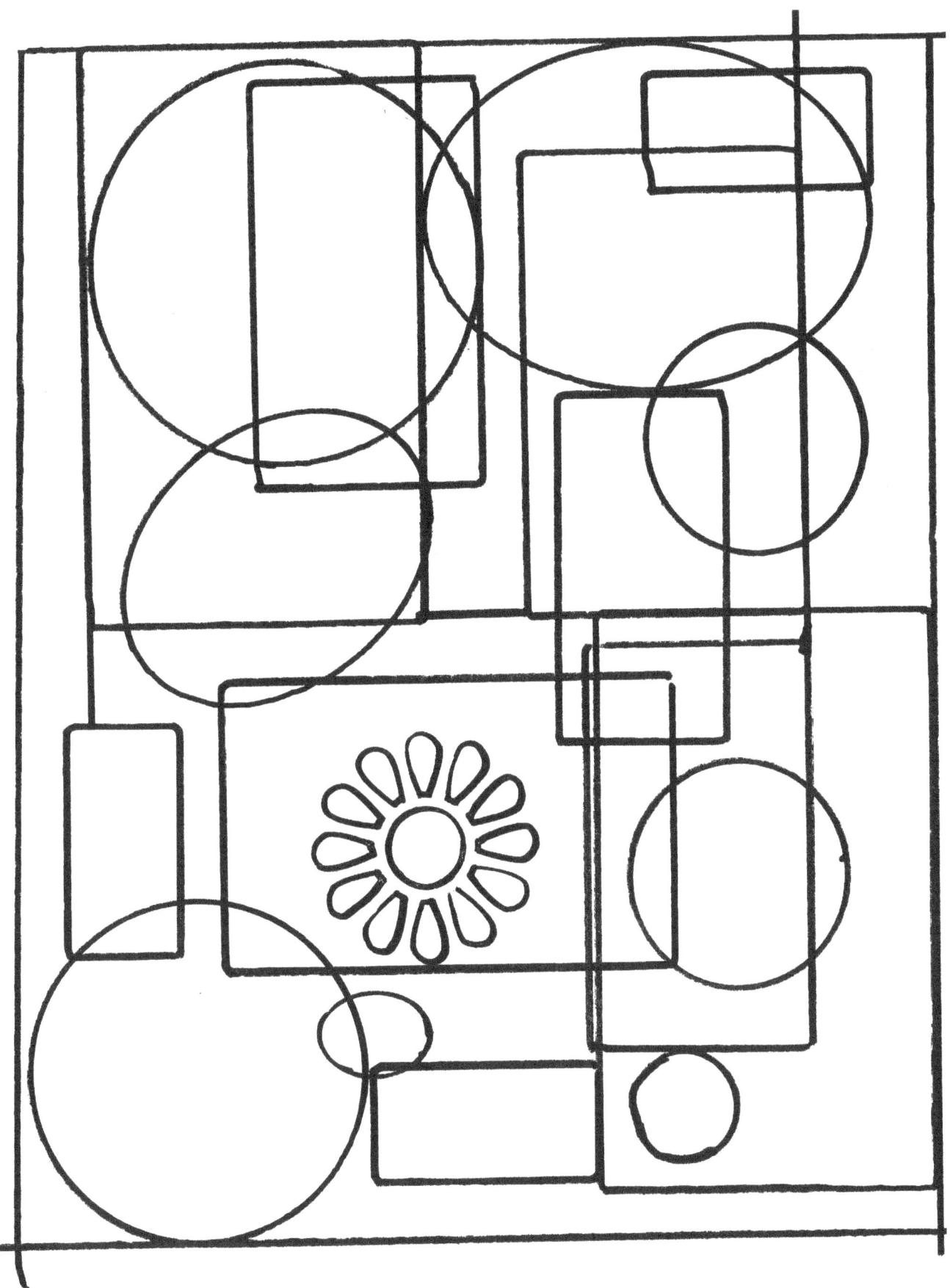

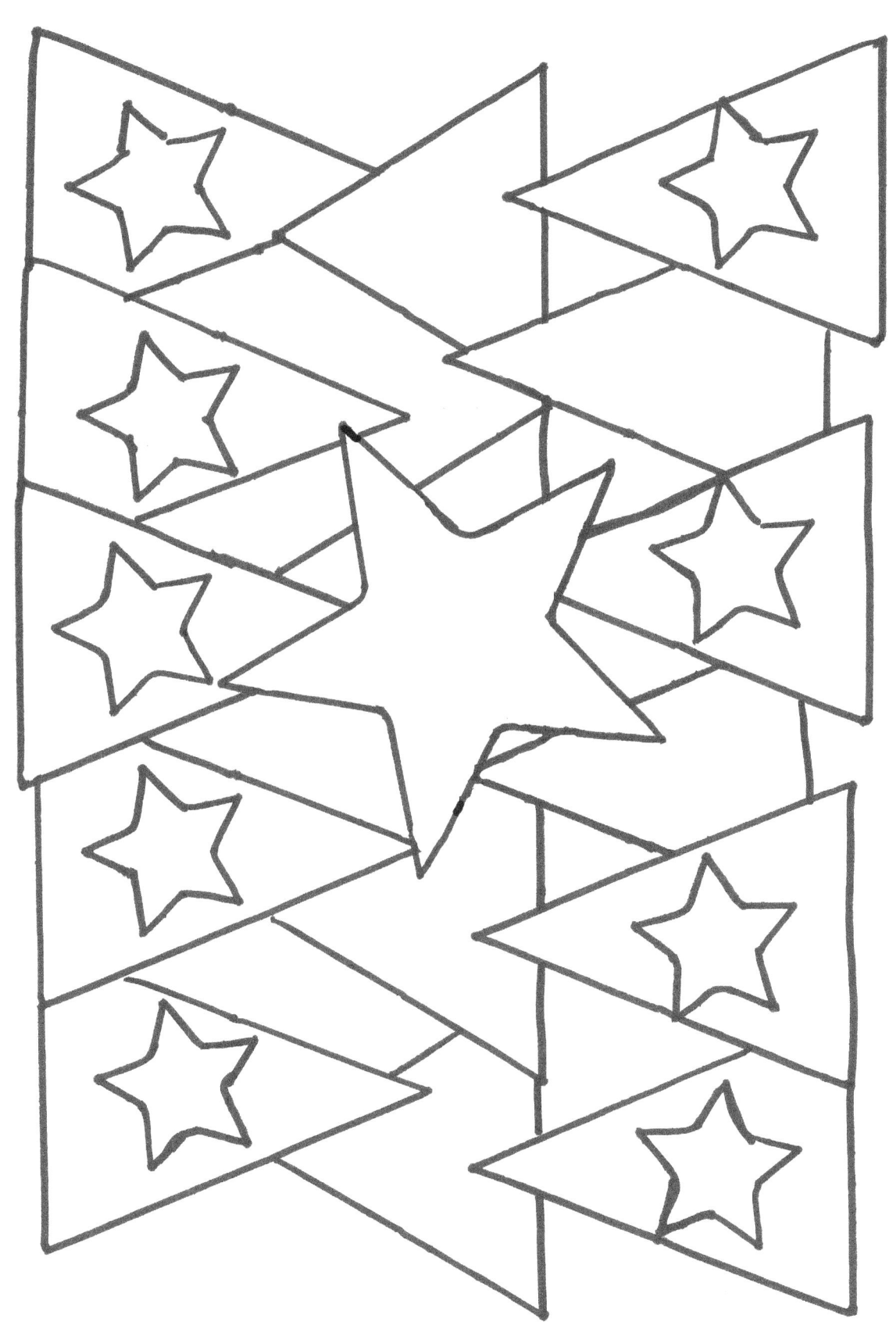

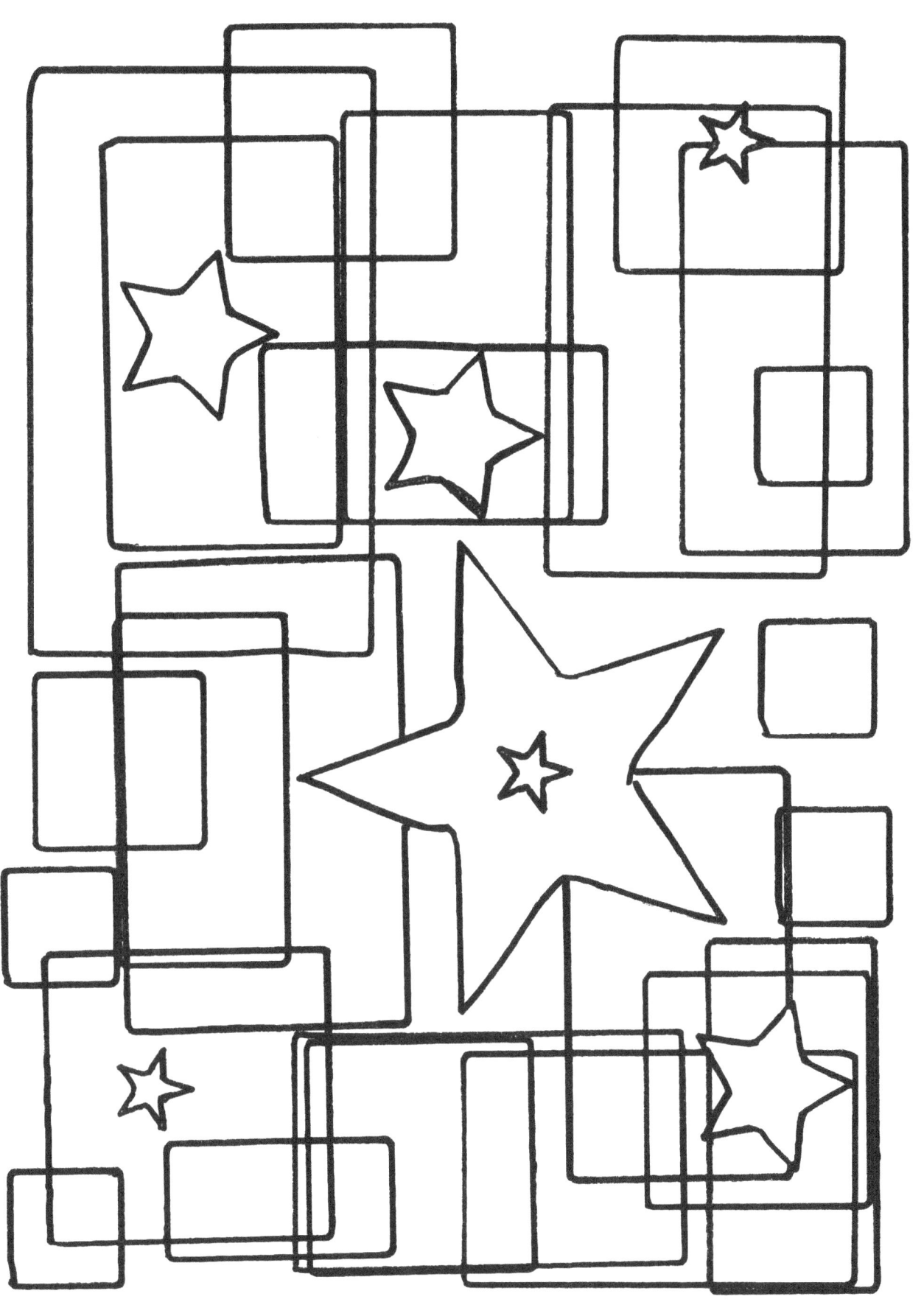

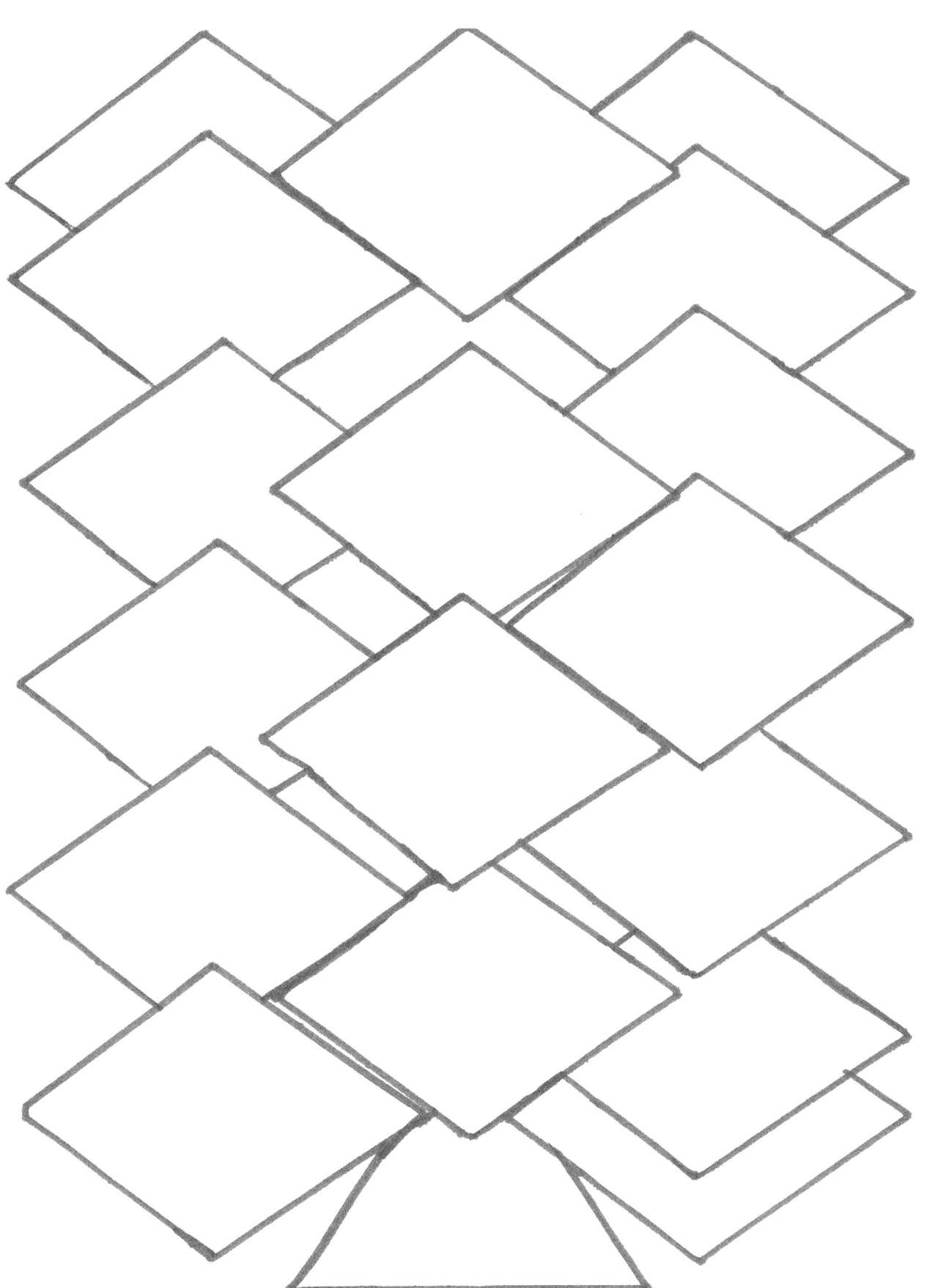

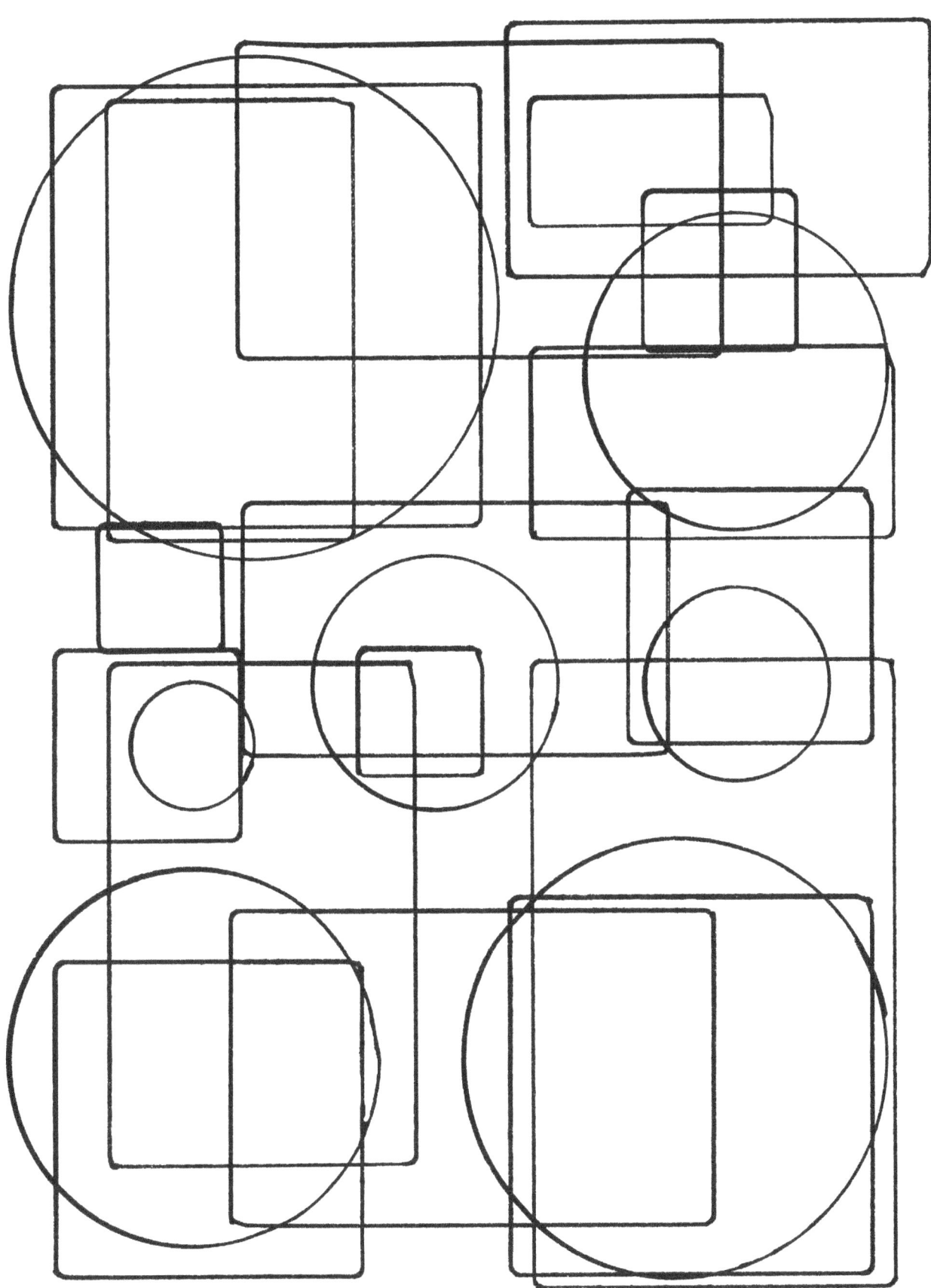

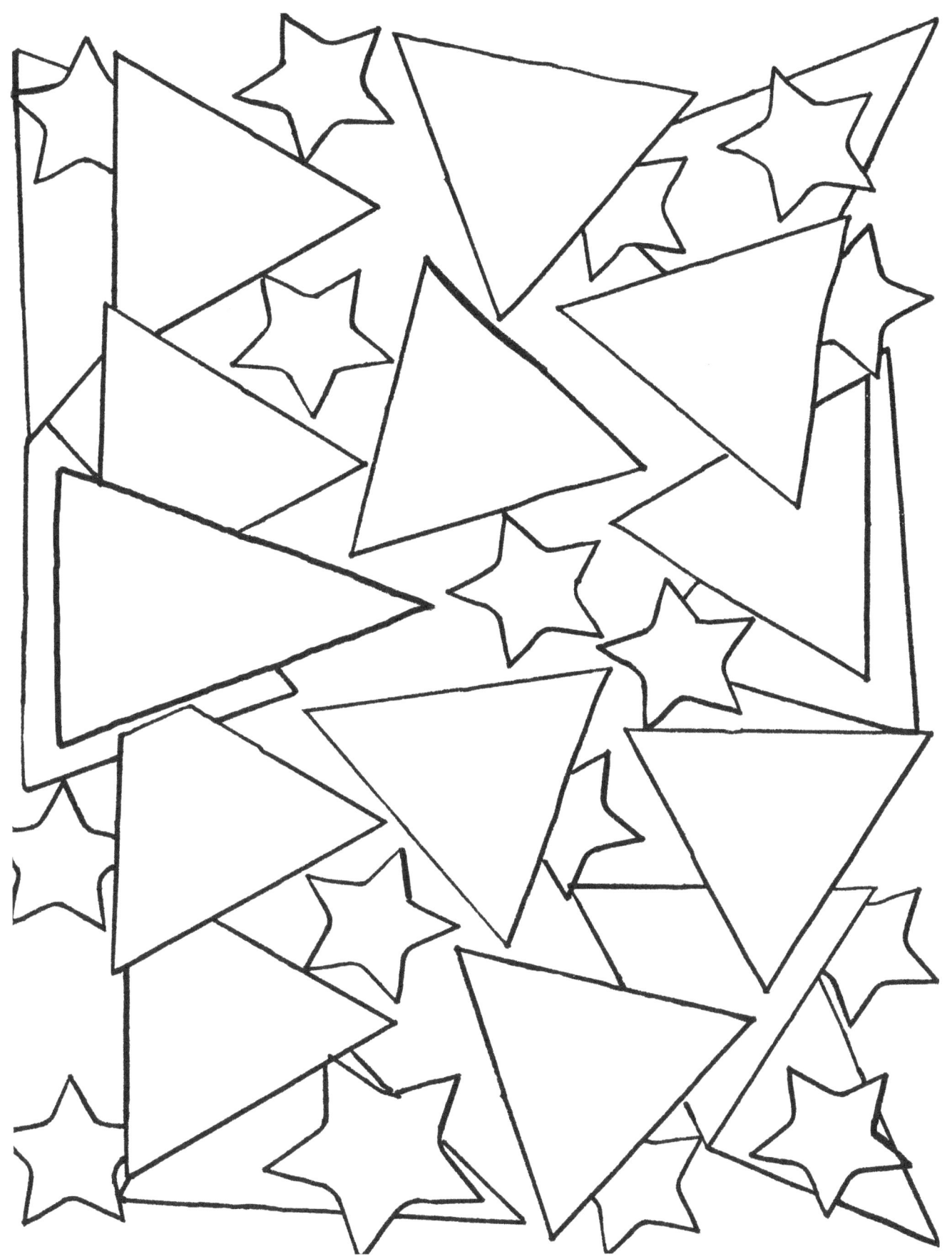

.

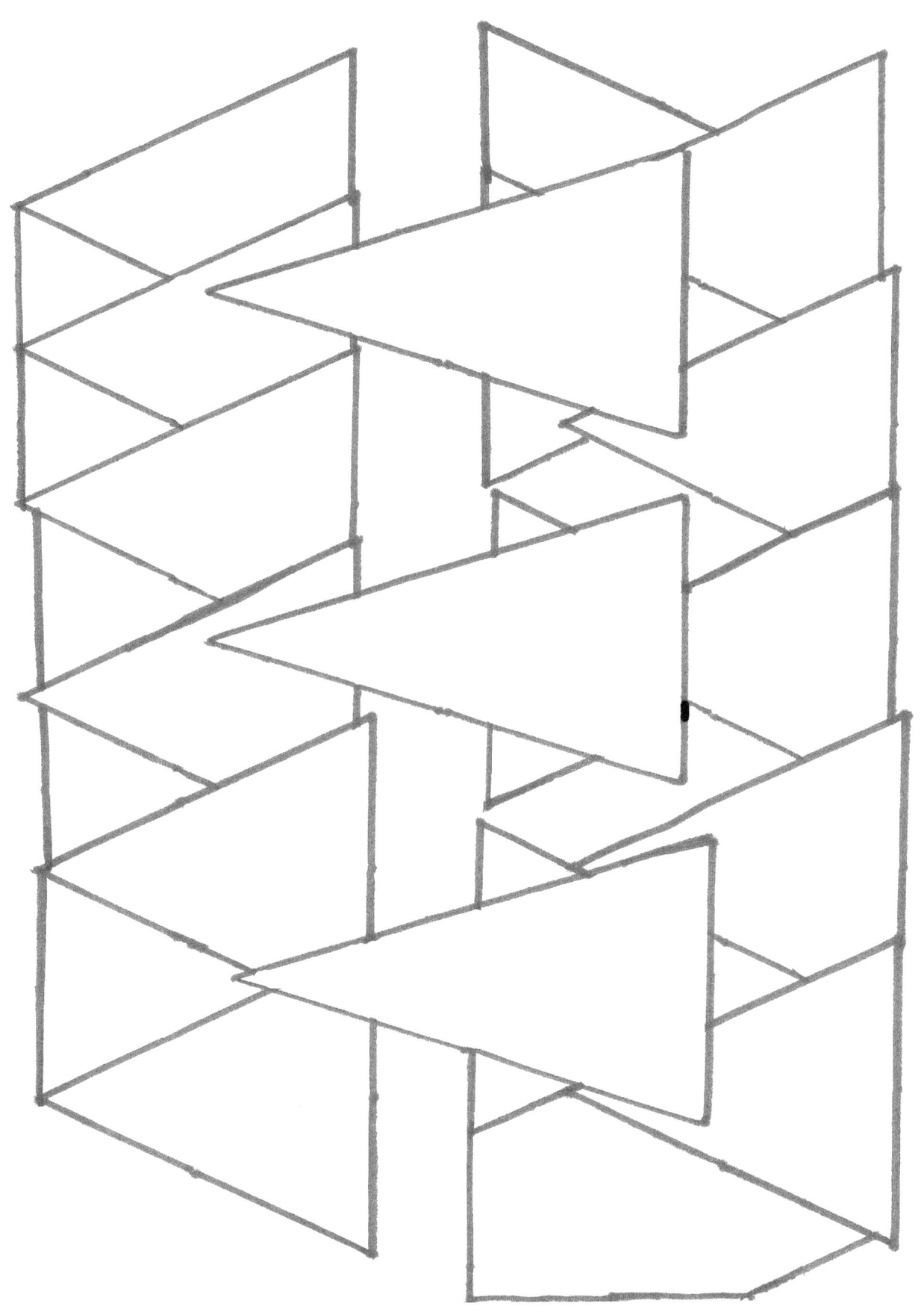

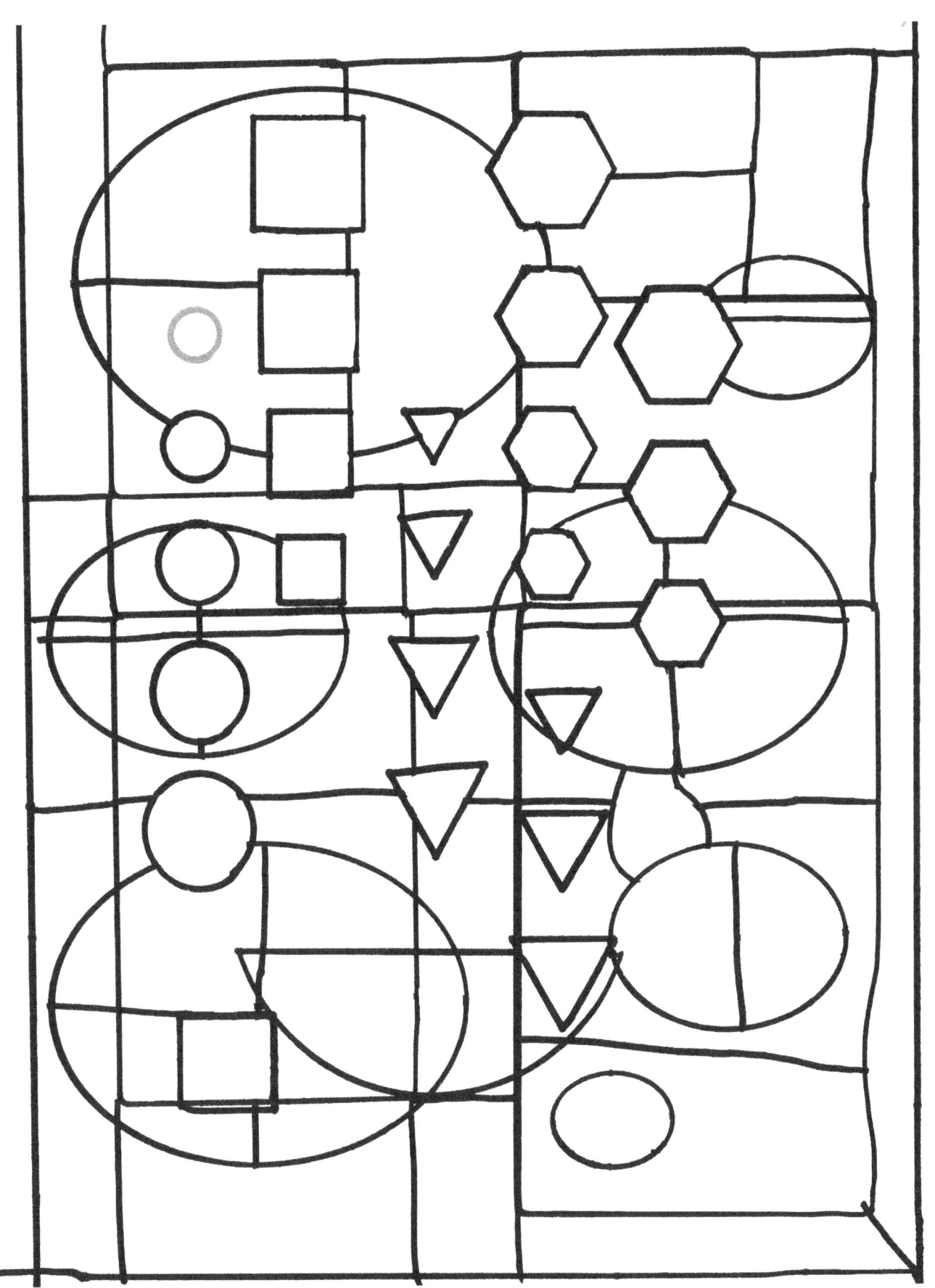

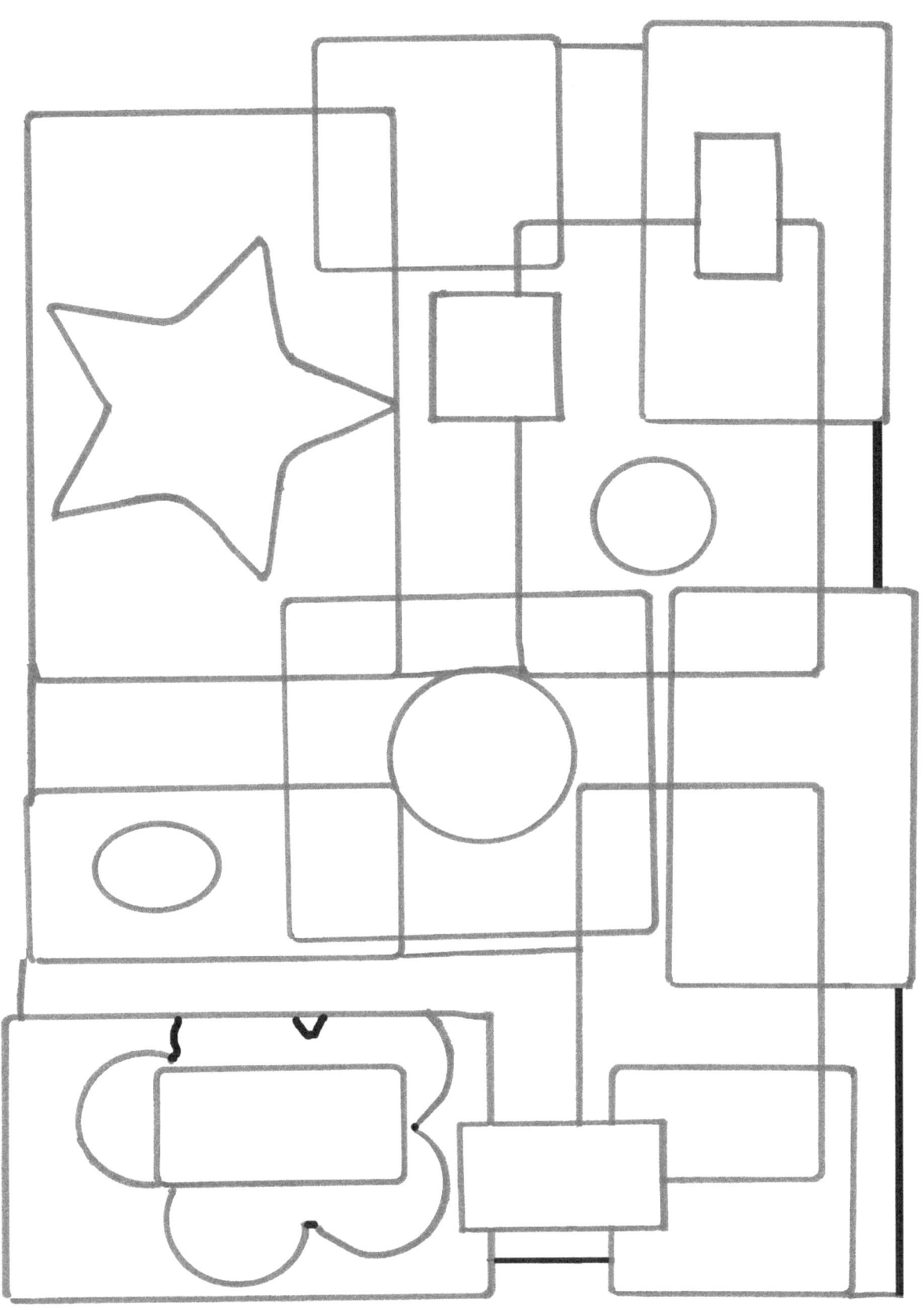

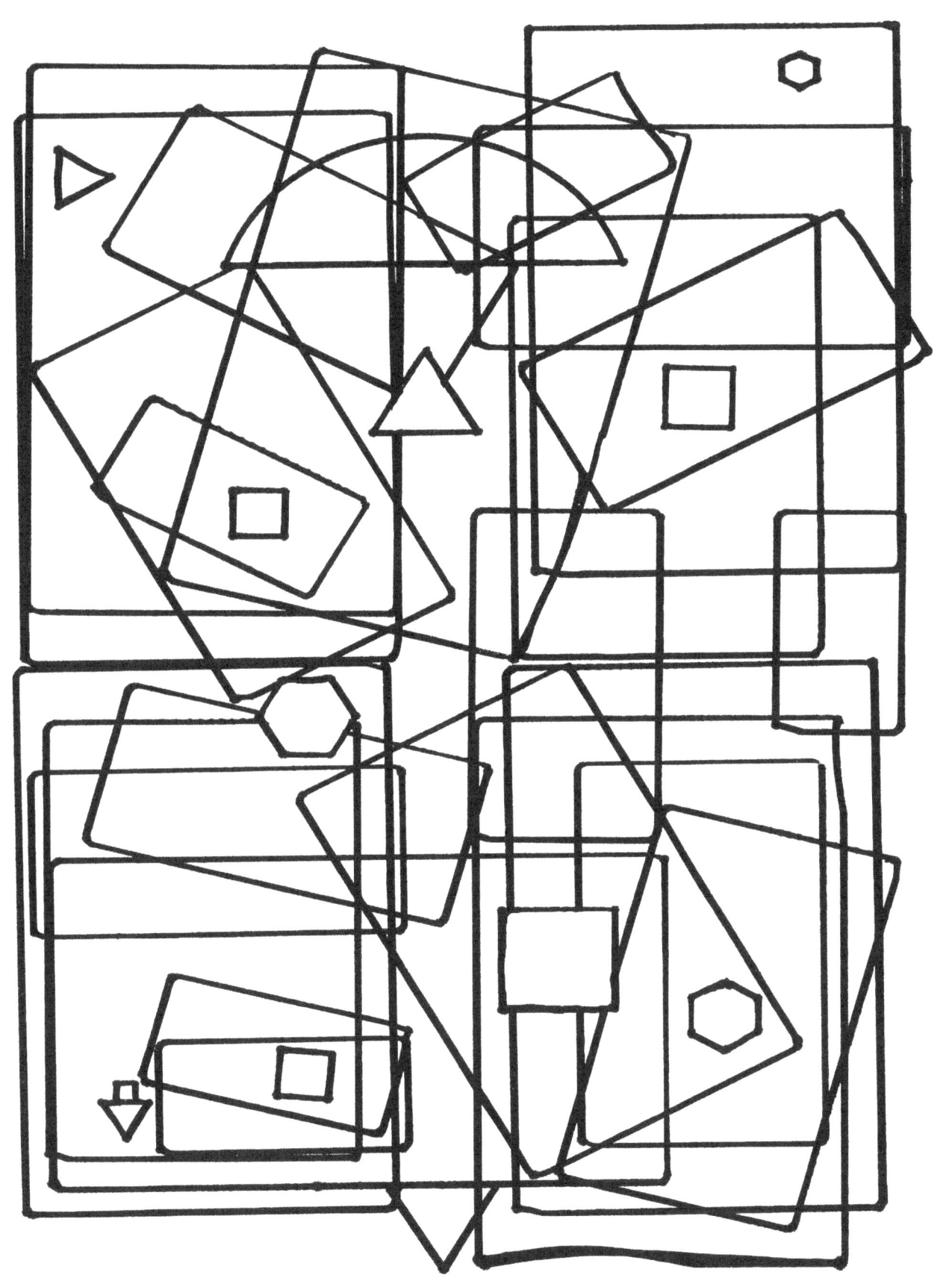

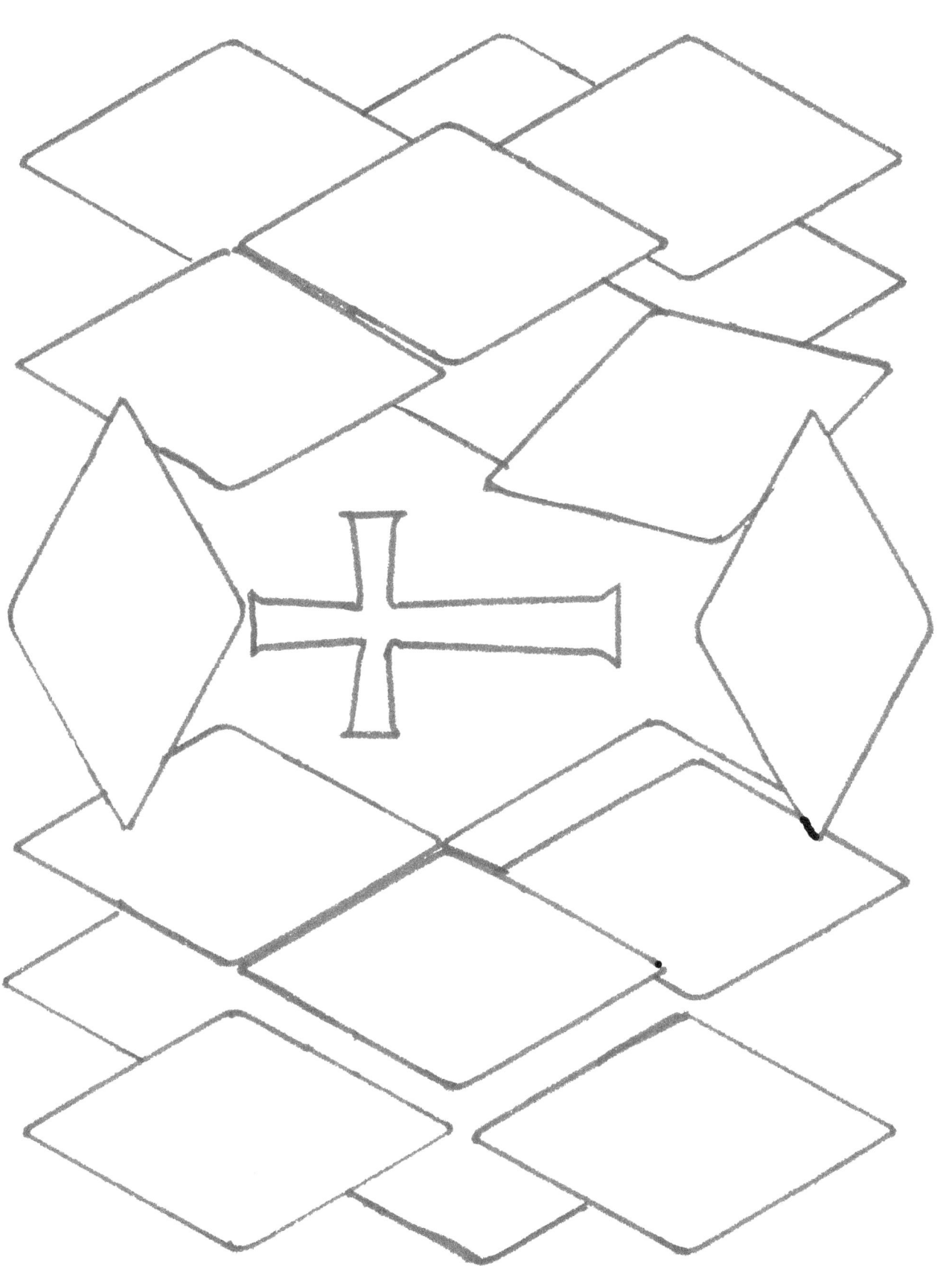

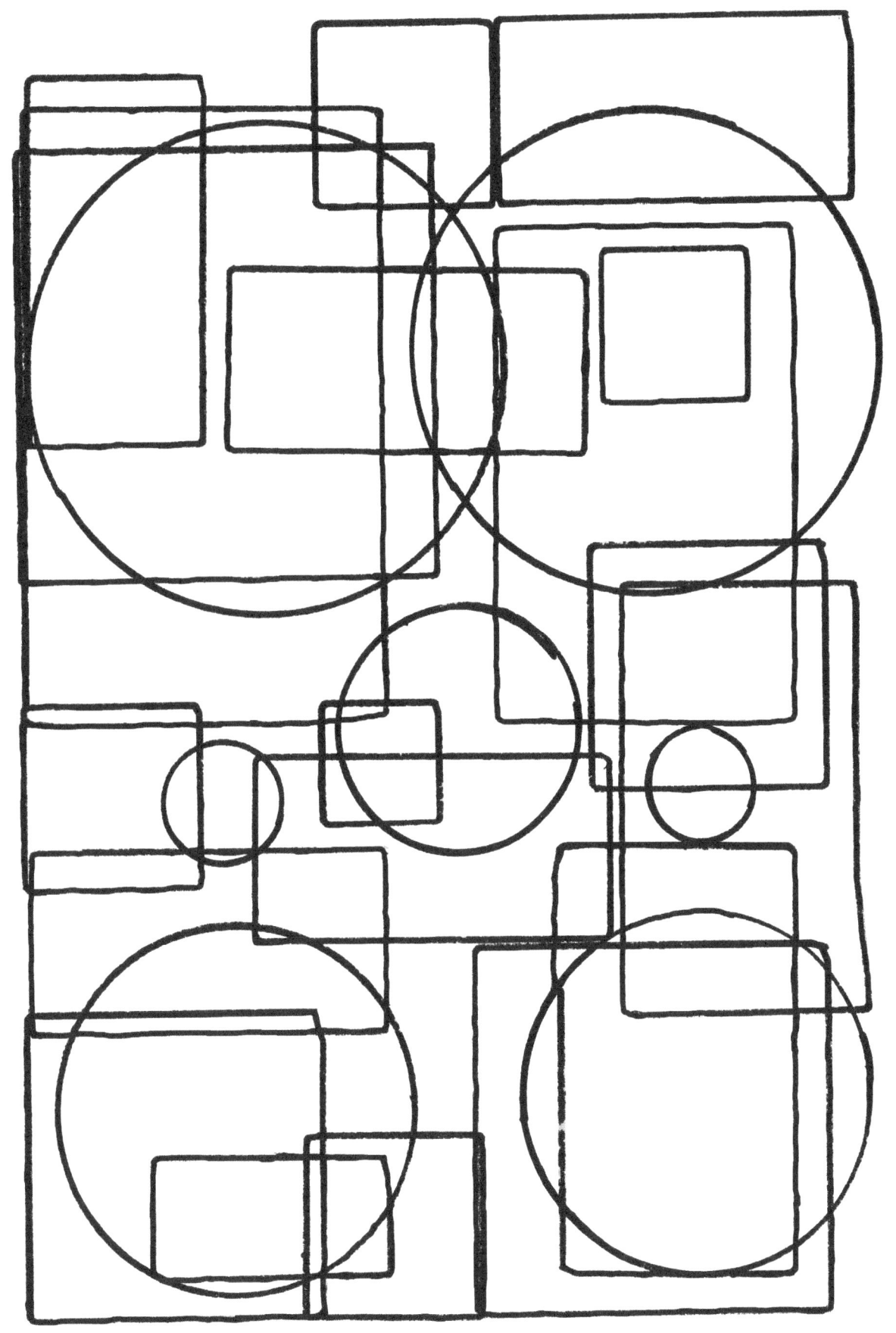

www.ingramcontent.com/pod-product-compliance
Lightning Source LLC
Chambersburg PA
CBHW080612180526
45168CB00007B/2881